CANADIAN ROCKIES

Text by
CARL BENN

Photographs by
ANDREA PISTOLESI

BONECHI

Distribution by
Canadian Souvenir Sales Ltd.

P.O. Box 250, Radium Hot Springs, B.C.,
Canada V0A 1M0

Ph: 250-347-9628
Fax: 250-347-9011   PH: 1 800 663 3834
Email cansou@telus.net   FAX: 1 888 590 2288

ISBN 1-895156-14-9

INDEX

INTRODUCTION	*Page 3*
MAP OF THE CANADIAN ROCKIES	" 128
Athabasca Falls	" 91
Athabasca Valley	" 100
Banff Avenue	" 11
BANFF NATIONAL PARK	" 7
Banff Springs Hotel	" 12
Bow Falls	" 17
Bow Lake	" 55
Bow River	" 17
Cameron Falls	" 118
Cameron Lake	" 119
Cascade Gardens	" 11
Castle Mountain	" 36
Cave and Basin Centennial Centre	" 21
Chateau Lake Louise	" 47
Columbia Icefield	" 82
Crowfoot Glacier	" 55
Emerald Lake	" 68
FAUNA	" 122
FLORA	" 126
GLACIER NATIONAL PARK	" 64
Hoodoos	" 17
Jasper town site	" 86
JASPER NATIONAL PARK	" 82
Jasper Park Lodge	" 90
Jasper Tramway	" 87
Johnston Canyon	" 32
KANANASKIS COUNTRY	" 76
KOOTENAY NATIONAL PARK	" 70
Kootenay River	" 73
Lake Louise	" 38
Lake Minnewanka	" 30
Maligne Canyon	" 103
Maligne Lake	" 109
Marble Canyon	" 75
Medicine Lake	" 105
Mistaya Canyon	" 62
Moraine Lake	" 51
Mount Assiniboine	" 79
Mount Chephren	" 60
Mount Edith Cavell	" 95
MOUNT ROBSON PROVINCIAL PARK	" 112
Mount Rundle	" 25
Num-ti-jah Lodge	" 56
Old Rail Station	" 48
Patricia Lake	" 99
Peyto Lake	" 56
Post Hotel	" 48
Prince of Wales Hotel	" 114
Pyramid Lake	" 98
Pyramid Mountain	" 97
Radium Hot Springs	" 70
Rafting	" 104
Red Rock Canyon	" 121
Saskatchewan River Crossing	" 60
Sinclair Canyon	" 70
Sulphur Mountain Gondola	" 22
Sunwapta Falls	" 91
Takakkaw Falls	" 65
Three Sisters	" 76
Trans-Canada Highway	" 80
Upper Hot Springs and Pool	" 24
Valley of the Ten Peaks	" 49
Vermilion Lakes	" 25
Victoria Glacier	" 38
Waterton Lakes	" 114
WATERTON LAKES NATIONAL PARK	" 114
Wenkchemna Peaks	" 49
YOHO NATIONAL PARK	" 65

CANADIAN ROCKIES
Project and editorial conception: Casa Editrice Bonechi
Publication Manager: Monica Bonechi
Picture research: Monica Bonechi
Cover, Graphic design and Make-up: Manuela Ranfagni
Editing: Anna Baldini

Text: Carl Benn
Maps: Stefano Benini

© Copyright by Casa Editrice Bonechi - Florence - Italy
E-mail: bonechi@bonechi.it - Internet: www.bonechi.it

ISBN 88-8029-793-7

*Photographs from archives of Casa Editrice Bonechi taken by
Andrea Pistolesi.*

*Photographs by courtesy of Canadian Souvenir Sales Ltd.:
pages 10 (below), 22 (below), 44 (above), 47 (below left), by John Bicknell;
pages 44 (below left and right), 47(below right), 78, 79, by Timothy G.M. Reynolds;
pages 69 (above), 112, 113 (below), 126, 127.*

* * *

INTRODUCTION

The magnificent Canadian Rockies are one of the world's most popular tourist destinations - and for good reason: they comprise some of the most glorious wilderness lands on earth, but they also are among the most accessible natural environments on the planet. At the same time, the very best in tourism facilities sit readily at hand to cater to a traveller's every need for comfort. Alternatively, those who feel like roughing it can find challenging opportunities to experience mountain and ice climbing, white water rafting, hiking, skiing, and camping in the wild within a few kilometres of the comforts of civilization.

The Rockies consist of several mountain groupings that run roughly along a northwest-southeast axis: the front ranges which lie beside the Alberta foothills, the eastern main ranges (such as those you will encounter at Lake Louise on the Alberta-British Columbia border), the western main ranges inside BC,

Takakkaw Falls, Canada's second tallest at 380 metres in Yoho National Park.

About 11,500 years ago, when the ice sheets were in retreat, the climate had begun to warm, and hunter-gatherer Palaeo-Indians started to appear at the southern and lower elevations of the Rocky Mountain and neighbouring regions. The environment they encountered below the mountains was a mix of tundra towards the north and lichen woodlands to the south.

They hunted such now-extinct beasts as ancient mammoths, mastodons, camels, horses, and sloths, as well as creatures indigenous to Canada today such as bison, beavers, and caribou. Gradually the more exotic species disappeared and the climate continued to warm to its present-day state.

The people themselves, ever numerous in the inhospitable environment of the Rockies, adapted to changing conditions and developed more complex and regionally-distinct societies

and the western ranges over by Radium Hot Springs on the border with the Rocky Mountain Trench. The story of the Rockies began hundreds of millions of years ago when the region lay under water. The land to the east drained into the sea, dumping sediment which slowly hardened into the distinctive layers of limestone, shale, dolomite, and quartzite that are so visible on the mountains today. Then, about 200 million years ago, the immense continental plate under North America began to move west and crashed into a series of islands, land masses, and other plates. Over the next 35 million years, these sedimentary layers were compressed horizontally. Subsequently, some of them broke under tremendous pressure and shifted up over the underlying layers, piling upwards, and forming mountains. Now, at an age of 120 million years, the Rockies are older than the Himalayas, the Alps, and the American Rockies. They also have been eroded significantly from the time of their primeval birth because the sedimentary rock that composes the mountains is susceptible to the forces of wind, water, and ice that have attacked these giant peaks over the millennia.

During the last of the ice ages, which ended about 11,000 years ago, most of Canada lay under massive sheets of ice. In the lowland areas, such as the Bow River Valley in Banff, glaciers transformed the landscape of the old 'V-shaped' river valleys by carving them deeper and wider so that most Rocky Mountain valleys today are more 'U-shaped' than they were before the glaciers descended upon the region.

over the centuries, as demonstrated by the changes in their tools which archaeologists have discovered in the Rockies and elsewhere in western Canada. The first Europeans to reach the Rocky Mountains encountered three main cultural groups, each comprising a number of different nations: the subarctic peoples to the north; and to the south, the plateau cultural group centred west of the mountains, and the inhabitants of the Great Plains to the east.

Before Europeans came to the Rockies, however, their goods arrived, carried here by aboriginal traders who acquired them from fur trade outposts at Hudson Bay and elsewhere. Similarly, modern horses reached the area in the early 1700s after making their way north from Spanish Mexico. By the 1750s, European explorers began to venture into what now is Alberta. Because of fierce competition between the Hudson's Bay Company of London and its rival, the North West Company in Montreal, fur trade posts began to be built in the province by the 1780s. Many fur trade employees married into aboriginal society and helped create a new, mixed-race cultural group, the Métis. In 1793, fur trader and explorer Alexander Mackenzie staked his claim to fame when he led the first group of Europeans through the Rockies from the plains to the Pacific Ocean. Christian missionaries arrived in Alberta in the early decades of the 19th century. Then, a trickle of ranchers and settlers moved onto the Alberta foothills east of the Rockies after the Canadian government negotiated treaties with the native inhabitants, beginning

in the 1870s. During this period of early exploration and settlement, however, the Rocky Mountains remained relatively quiet.

That changed with the arrival of the railway in the 1880s. Earlier, in 1867, far to the east, the older British colonies of Nova Scotia, New Brunswick, and the United Province of Canada (now Ontario and Quebec) united as the Dominion of Canada, a country within the British Empire. Two years later, the Dominion purchased the vast Hudson's Bay Company territory representing what now forms part of northern Quebec and Ontario, the totality of Manitoba, Saskatchewan, and Alberta, and much of the Yukon and Northwest Territories. Then, in 1871, British Columbia joined the Canadian confederation. However, there was a condition: a transcontinental railway had to be built linking it to the rest of Canada through the Rocky Mountains. In 1883, that railway, the celebrated Canadian Pacific, reached Banff from the east. Work continued for another two years, and in November 1885, the last spike of the transcontinental railway was driven into the ground at Craigellachie in the Eagle Pass of British Columbia. The first train to make the journey from eastern Canada to the Pacific left Montreal in June 1886. Afterwards, large numbers of settlers, miners, and others moved to Alberta and British Columbia and began the process of creating the modern society that now is home to the

Lake Louise, a glorious spot in Banff National Park.

Pretty Peyto Lake on the Icefields Parkway between Banff and Jasper.

several million people who live in Canada's two west-ernmost provinces.

The advent of the railway allowed for the birth of mining and forestry in the Rockies. With good rail connections, coal mining and logging became major activities at Banff and Jasper in late Victorian times, while talc, iron, lead, silver, zinc, gold, sulphur, and other minerals encouraged miners to set up operations throughout the Rocky Mountains. Tourism also got its birth in the 1880s because of the railways. Now, travel-trade is the central industry in Banff, Jasper, and much of the rest of the Canadian Rocky Mountains.

Today, the region is well positioned to provide you with all the tourist facilities you will ever need while you enjoy the primary attractions of the Rockies, the stunningly grand scenery and one of the world's great wildernesses. The best of the Rockies is preserved in perpetuity in a number of famous and not-so-famous national and provincial parks.

So important are the Canadian Rocky Mountains to the planet that the United Nations declared them to be a world heritage site in 1984.

Now, at this point in our story, we would like to invite you to join us on a journey through the Canadian Rocky Mountains, to peruse the pages below and enjoy our wonderful photographs, as we explore this fascinating part of the world.

Beautiful poppies on the grounds of the Chateau Lake Louise.

Athabasca Falls, one of Jasper National Park's many attractions.

BANFF NATIONAL PARK

Banff, Alberta sits on the Trans-Canada Highway, 130 kilometres west of Calgary. Founded in 1885, it is Canada's oldest national park. Two years earlier, some railway workers improvised a rough ladder out of a tree to explore a cave that the local natives had used for generations to cure bodily complaints. Inside, the three men discovered sulphurous hot springs which, they realized, had commercial value in an age when 'taking the waters' was a fashionable treatment for whatever ailed people. They built a log cabin nearby, and within a year several small enterprises had opened to cater to guests who wanted to test the restorative powers of the springs. However, arguments arose over who owned Banff's resources. The Canadian government, therefore, created Rocky Mountain Park in a 26-square-kilometre area around the springs to keep them in the public domain. Gradually, the park grew to take in the region's most scenic areas, eventually reaching the 6641 square kilometres encompassed by today's Banff National Park.

The most visible industry in Banff today is tourism. Back in 1888, the general manager of the Canadian Pacific Railway, William Cornelius Van Horne, helped foster that industry when he opened the magnificent Banff Springs Hotel. In Van Horne's view, tourists not only would spend their money eating and sleeping in his hotel, but would take his trains across the country to get here, and thereby rescue the near-bankrupt CPR, and even help the railway prosper. He knew that Banff had the key ingredients to attract affluent Victorian tourists: beautiful scenery, curative hot springs, and the opportunity to indulge in the era's increasingly-popular avocation, 'alpinism,' in which people sought out spectacular mountain environments to increase their knowledge of exotic landscapes and to find transcendence amidst nature's cold and sublimely hostile peaks.

The Banff town site with the baronial Banff Springs Hotel in the background.

This and following pages: overview of Banff in the Bow River Valley, the most popular tourist destination in the Rockies.

BANFF AVENUE

The heart of Banff National Park today is the town of Banff, a community of 7000. Each year four million guests drop in to visit. If you come during the peak winter or summer seasons, you might be forgiven for thinking that every one of them is in town at the same moment as you are while you wait impatiently at the end of a long queue to get a seat in a restaurant or buy an ice cream cone! (A hint: late spring and early autumn are less crowded.) The name of the town and park was a conceit to the two largest shareholders of the Canadian Pacific Railway in the 19th century, Donald Smith and George Stephen, both of whom hailed from Banffshire (now Grampian) in Scotland.

The town's main street is Banff Avenue with its dozens of gift and souvenir shops, restaurants, clubs, and services. Many of the shops sell upscale merchandise, and there are several commercial galleries specializing in native and western art. One of the stores is the Hudson's Bay Company outlet. The HBC had its origins in a royal charter from King Charles II in 1670 to trade furs in and out of Hudson Bay. While the history of the HBC was once the stuff of legend, 'the Bay' now survives primarily as a department store chain. Yet memories of its glory days can be found in its shop where you can purchase such historic items as the famous 'point blankets' of fur trade renown.

CASCADE GARDENS

The administrative centre for Banff is situated in the charming Cascade Gardens at the foot of Banff Avenue. Here, you can enjoy a shaded and flower-filled respite from the bustle of the town, catch your breath, and get the travel information you need to enjoy your Rocky Mountain vacation. Alternatively, you can look back up Banff Avenue towards Cascade Mountain and snap one of the most popular pictures in the Rockies. Developed in the 1930s as a make-work project during the Great Depression, the gardens are just one of a number of interesting attractions in the town. Another is the Buffalo Paddock near the Trans-Canada Highway. There are two kinds of bison (or buffalo) in North America, the wood bison native to this part of the country, and the more famous plains bison. Sadly, the last of the wood bison in the Rockies was killed in 1858 near Lake Louise. The bison you see today are descended from ones shipped in from Wood Buffalo National Park far to the northeast. Rainy-day visitors can fill a few hours at one of Banff's museums: the Park Museum, the Natural History Museum, the Whyte Museum of the Canadian Rockies, and the Luxton Museum which surveys the region's aboriginal story. Culture vultures will enjoy the Banff Centre which offers artistic exhibits, dramatic performances, and music festivals.

Banff Avenue in summer and winter, with Cascade Mountain in the background. Below: gorgeous floral colour abounds at the Cascade Gardens.

BANFF SPRINGS HOTEL

The most prominent human landmark in the Rockies is the Banff Springs Hotel. When new in 1888, it was the world's largest hotel at 250 rooms. Back then, a day's stay cost $3.50. Designed by architect Bruce Price, the Banff Springs was the first of a number of chateau-like hotels the Canadian Pacific Railway would build across Canada. During its first season, it hosted upwards of 5000 guests. That number steadily rose, reaching 10,000 in 1904.

Gradually, the CPR replaced the original building with a new one constructed in the Scottish baronial tradition between 1910 and 1928. As might be expected, the Banff Springs was the address of choice in the Rockies. Therefore, it played host to all sorts of famous people, including heads of state, royalty, and those royals of popular culture, movie stars. Recently renovated by Canadian Pacific Hotels, the Banff Springs can lodge 1700 guests in its 825 rooms who are pampered with superlative services, a spa, good restaurants, comfortable lounges, interesting shops, an Olympic-sized pool, tennis courts, stables, and skating facilities. Even if you're not a guest, don't be shy about visiting and enjoying the hotel grounds and public areas.

The Banff Springs Hotel, a Bow River landmark at the base of Sulphur Mountain since 1888.

Open to the public, the golf course at the Banff Springs Hotel offers one of the world's most scenic rounds of golf. Built with prisoner-of-war labour during World War I, it was redesigned in 1927.

The Bow Falls in the town of Banff near the Banff Springs Hotel. Above: Hoodoos at Tunnel Mountain.

Following pages: the majestic Bow River, just one of the many waterways where you can experience a rafting tour.

BOW RIVER AND FALLS

The town of Banff sits in the Bow Valley between Sulphur and Cascade mountains. The river that cuts through the town is the mighty Bow, which flows 645 kilometres from the glacially-fed waters of Bow Lake, through Banff, and off through Calgary to join the Oldman River. As well as mighty, it's murky too because of glacial till in its waters. In total, it drains an area of 25,300 square kilometres. A popular destination along the river is the Bow Falls, located near the Banff Springs Hotel.

One of the best ways of seeing the Bow River is on a guided, family-oriented rafting trip provided by a commercial operator in the town. This business is just one of hundreds in the Rockies that makes its money from supplying tourists with the services they desire. Thus, the Rockies offer bike and boat rentals, cruises, carriage tours, fishing, golf, horseback riding, kayak and whitewater rafting, and all sorts of outfitting and guided trail tours.

Various forms of accommodation, from primitive campsites to grand hotels, satisfy every taste, and some of Canada's best dining establishments, along with interesting ethnic restaurants, are to be found throughout the region.

HOODOOS

Some of the weirdest rock configurations in the Rockies, visible at such places as Yoho and Banff national parks, are Hoodoos. Typically fashioned from layers of shale and sandstone, these missile-like formations are carved out of the earth by a mix of erosion, wind, rain, and surface water. They range in size from a few humble centimetres to more majestic heights of several metres. Often they are capped with an odd-looking hard rock top which protects the lower parts from deterioration. Once the cap disappears, the hoodoo is doomed to rapid erosion. One legend claims that hoodoos are giants who have been turned to stone, only to awake at night and frighten people by throwing rocks at them. Another asserts that they are teepees inhabited by evil spirits. In the Banff region, you can see four sets of hoodoos with little difficulty. One is located at Tunnel Mountain, another near Canmore, a third at Lake Minnewanka, and a fourth, incomplete set, sits near the Cascade hydro-electric facility. The ones at Lake Minnewanka still have their caps on, while those at Tunnel Mountain are accessible along a short interpretive hiking trail. If you plan to visit other parts of the province, you can find particularly striking hoodoos in the Alberta Badlands.

Inside the cave that gave birth to western Canada's tourism industry. Above: the pool restored to its 1912 appearance.

CAVE AND BASIN CENTENNIAL CENTRE

The cave and basin, discovered in 1883 by three railway workers, are the literal source of the creation of Banff National Park. Back in the late 19th and early 20th centuries, people flocked to the 34-degree-Celsius springs for their supposed curative and restorative powers, and in some cases, just for a hot bath in a world without much plumbing! Shortly after their discovery, the springs offered bath houses and other conveniences where, for 10 cents, people could unwind from the stresses of the Victorian world. In 1888, over 5000 people swam in the waters at the Cave and Basin. Because of intense demand, the government built new facilities beside the cave between 1912 and 1914, including what then was Canada's largest swimming pool.

Sadly, the original cave and basin, along with the pool, gradually became structurally unsound and had to be closed in 1976. With many people disappointed by this unfortunate event, the federal government restored the Cave and Basin, rebuilt the pool to the 1912 design, and recreated an 1886 bath house to add to the historical interest. In 1985, the Cave and Basin Centennial Centre opened to honour the 100th anniversary of the national park system. Now it hosts over a million visitors every year to the historic cave and basin area (open all year).

You can tour the cave and basin and inside these renowned attractions, you will see the original space that the railway workers found in the 1880s, looking much the way it did back then, complete with foul-smelling, sulphurous hot water. You also will see the strange sponge-like calcite rock that dominates the interior, known as tufa, which at some places is seven metres thick. Audio-visual presentations, historical displays, and geological exhibits interpret the story of this curious place. The Cave and Basin complex also boasts a tea room, a terraced picnic area, and the inevitable gift shop. You can enjoy short walks from the centre to explore the cave's immediate surroundings. One visits a nearby marshland to consider how the heated spring water has affected the surrounding ecosystems. Another is a wheelchair-accessible path that takes people to the cave's famous vent opening.

Banff from the gondola; lower: gondola arriving at the summit.
Opposite, upper: Canada's highest restaurant; bottom: the
mountain-top boardwalk.

SULPHUR MOUNTAIN GONDOLA

Sulphur Mountain gets its name from the smell of the hot springs near its base. At 2451 metres, this is a popular peak with visitors since it is easily accessible via gondola. The lift, built in 1959, is one of several in Banff National Park. It whisks you to an elevation of 2285 metres in eight minutes inside roomy, safe, and glass-enclosed gondolas while you gaze out at a sensational 360-degree view of Banff, Cascade Mountain, and the surrounding area. Once at the summit, you can savour the mountain top environment that normally is so hard to reach, while admiring breathtaking views of the Bow River Valley, Lake Minnewanka, and the neighbouring mountains. You can even have dinner at Canada's highest restaurant!

Brown bighorn sheep live on the mountain and may approach you looking for a tasty handout. However, feeding them is not allowed. The largest of these animals weighs about 125 kilograms and stands a metre tall at the shoulders. Typically, they travel in flocks of up to 50 animals under the leadership of a dominant and mature ram, whose position is determined in duels with other rams. While his place in the hierarchy is challenged regularly, the dominant ewe, who decides where the lambs and other ewes will travel during the summer months, often reigns unchallenged for many years.

UPPER HOT SPRINGS AND POOL

The Upper Hot Springs, which have attracted tourists since the 1880s, are situated a short distance from downtown Banff. Fed by the naturally-heated springs of Sulphur Mountain to about 40 degrees Celsius, they provide patrons with a hotter soak than the waters of the more famous Cave and Basin.

Commercial use of these springs began in 1886 when a CPR doctor, R.G. Brett, opened a 'sanitorium,' with water piped from Sulphur Mountain 2400 metres away. Claiming the water could cure almost every complaint, Brett charged what then was a hefty $2.00 a day to use his facilities. At the same time, he built the Grandview Villa right at the Upper Hot Springs themselves where he offered billiards, massages, and non-alcoholic 'temperance' drinks along with his water cures. At one point, canes and crutches were nailed up on the trees at the springs, supposedly by people who no longer needed them after taking the waters. In 1901, Dr Brett's villa at the springs burned to the ground and the Canadian government decided that subsequent development would take place under public control, although it did not build the present structure until the 1930s. Meanwhile, Dr Brett's sanitorium burned in 1933 and now is the site of the Cascade Gardens.

The Upper Hot Springs, recently renovated, draw thousands of visitors wanting to de-stress themselves. The outdoor pool, with its reasonable entry fee, is particularly popular. Those with a bit more money to spend will enjoy the spa facilities with offerings ranging from aromatherapy to mineral water plunges. The pool's hot water can be enjoyed in winter as well as summer even though the surrounding air temperature can be more than a little nippy. Interpretive exhibits explain the history of the springs. Facilities for disabled travellers along with a cafe, patio, and shops fill out the services available at this venerable attraction. If you would like to explore undeveloped hot springs, then the Middle Hot Springs above the Banff town site, not far from the Upper Springs, are a good place to go. They can be reached via a three-kilometre walk from the Cascade Gardens up Sulphur Mountain. Once here, you will find a cave and the typical tufa rock found in a natural setting along with some majestic views to reward you for your climb up the mountain.

Upper Hot Springs and Pool, a good place to sooth your aching limbs after a vigorous mountain hike.

The shallow Vermilion Lakes, near the Banff town site.

Following four pages: the Vermilion Lakes with Mount Rundle in the background, as enjoyed through the light and shadow of an evolving day.

VERMILION LAKES AND MOUNT RUNDLE

The Vermilion Lakes, an extensive region of montane wetlands, lie west of the Banff town site. Their name comes from ochre beds at the iron-rich mineral springs at the Vermilion River pass where the Blackfoot and Kootenay tribes obtained materials for some of their ceremonial body paints. At one point in the past, the national parks staff used dams to keep the lake levels high enough to support boating and fishing. More recently, they removed the dams to reduce the degree of human intervention in the environment. The lakes subsequently dropped so that they now are quite shallow and the surrounding region has begun to fill in with aquatic vegetation.

This development is the normal first step in the evolution from a montane wetland to a floodplain forest, a process that should be completed within the next few hundred years. Nearby is the Fenland Trail, a two-kilometre path through floodplain forest which presents you with an opportunity to see what the Vermilion Lakes will look like in the future. This trail is just one of 80 at Banff which traverse 1300 kilometres of the park to take you off through all kinds of fascinating ecological zones.

At 2949 metres, Mount Rundle stands proudly behind the Vermilion Lakes. It got its name in 1859 to honour Robert Rundle, an English Methodist missionary who worked among the plains tribes in the 1840s. Located between Canmore and the Banff townsite, it probably is the most famous mountain in Banff. It and another celebrated local peak, Castle Mountain, are good examples of the two dominant mountain forms in the park. Mount Rundle presents the typical configuration of the front ranges of the Rockies, with its slanting table-top shape. Castle Mountain is characteristic of the castellated main ranges with its layer-cake profile.

The Canadian Rockies start at the southern end of British Columbia and Alberta and extend north 1200 kilometres to the Liard River Basin near the Yukon Territory. At the centre of the Rockies is the Continental (or Great) Divide. Here, the height of land separates Canada into two primary parts: a westerly portion which drains rivers into the Pacific Ocean; and an easterly division which sends water to the Arctic and Atlantic oceans.

The divide also acts as much of the border between BC and Alberta. The cattle country of Alberta's rolling foothills lies east of the Rockies about 1000 to 1500 metres below the mountains. The foothills eventually join the vast grain-growing regions of the Canadian prairies at an average distance of 50 kilometres from the Rocky Mountains.

LAKE MINNEWANKA

Lake Minnewanka, a bit northeast of downtown Banff, is the largest body of water in the park. Its name comes from the Cree expression for 'lake of the water spirit.' Today, it is larger than it was in historical times because the outlet of the original lake was dammed in 1912, and in 1941 the lake was enlarged further. A good way to see the lake and surrounding region is along the Lake Minnewanka Loop, a 25-kilometre drive past Cascade Mountain and other interesting sites.

There are several recreational opportunities at the lake to amuse you today. Fishing is popular, particularly as this lake is the only one in Banff where power boats are allowed. There is also a 90-minute boat tour you can take to view the sights and wildlife. If scuba diving is your thing, you can visit the site of a former resort, Minnewanka Landing, that now lies submerged below the waters as a result of the lake's 20th-century expansions. (The lake is 25 metres higher than it was before damming.)

Looking across Lake Minnewanka you can see the Palliser Range of Mountains, named after Captain John Palliser. Back in 1857, this Irish-born explorer led a three-year scientific expedition to the Canadian west on behalf of the British government. His objectives were to determine if this poorly understood region could be settled and whether or not roads and railways could be cut through the Rockies to link the British territories in North America from the Atlantic to the Pacific. The result of his journey was the first large scale scientific report on the Canadian west. One of its conclusions was that the immense interior east of the Rockies could sustain an agricultural population. That news subsequently helped both the British and Canadian governments plan to end Hudson's Bay Company control over the region and open it up to settlement.

Between the Banff townsite and Lake Minnewanka is the site of the former town of Bankhead, a coal mining community that existed between 1903 and 1922. Here, you can imagine what life was like back then by following an interpretive trail that passes through the site. The buildings are mostly gone now, but in its glory days it boasted 40 homes, two large boarding houses, a church, a school, and sporting facilities to cater to the 600 people who lived and worked in Bankhead. The population at the time consisted largely of immigrant workers from Germany, Poland, Italy, and China. When the town closed, the buildings were sold off and moved. Some survive today in the Banff town site.

In and around pretty Lake Minnewanka.

This and following three pages: Johnston Canyon, a great place to explore en route from Banff to Lake Louise.

JOHNSTON CANYON

There are two ways to travel north from the Banff town site to Lake Louise: the Trans-Canada Highway and the Bow Valley Parkway. The latter is the more relaxed and scenic route and will take you past such popular attractions as Johnston Canyon and Castle Mountain. En route, you will pass through hilly terrain known as the Hillsdale Slide. About 8000 years ago, a large part of a mountain collapsed to form the hills you see today. This happened after the mountain had been undermined thousands of years earlier during the last ice age. Geologists have documented the site as one of the Rockies' largest landslides.

Johnston Canyon, about 25 kilometres north of the Banff town site, is well worth a stop along the parkway. This land form, roughly 30 metres deep, and as narrow as six metres wide in places, is accessible along a good walkway that takes you past seven waterfalls, including the 30-metre upper falls, and allows you to explore how water erodes rock over many centuries. Along the way you can see a grouping of six springs, the Inkpots, coloured a deep aqua by glacial sediments. The hike to the Inkpots can take four hours; so if you don't have the time, you might limit your walking to a trip to the lower falls at 1.5 kilometres from the parkway. The route takes you across a number of catwalks which jut right out into the gorge where you will be splashed by the spray from the cataracts. One of the attractions at the canyon, as in the Rockies as a whole, is the profusion of pretty wildflowers you will encounter. Like many trails in the national parks system, you'll find interpretive plaques along the way to make your visit more enjoyable by explaining details about the environment to you.

Many tourists to Canada come with strange notions about it always being cold here. Summer in much of Canada can be downright hot with 30 degrees Celsius, or more, being fairly common depending on where you visit.

Because of the elevation of the Rockies, however, things are a bit unusual here. One summer day might hit 30 degrees; but then, it might snow the next. And, because the mountains sometimes create their own micro environments, it might be bright and sunny where you are but pour rain a kilometre away. Spring here tends to come late; autumn can be glorious with bright cool days.

Winter comes early in the Rockies, with average daytime temperatures in January hovering around minus 15 but with some cold snaps dropping the mercury to minus 35 or 40. Wind chill makes it seem colder. In any case, the weather changes rapidly and frequently, so be prepared.

Castle Mountain on the Bow River was known as Eisenhower Mountain between 1946 and 1979.

CASTLE MOUNTAIN

On the way to Lake Louise from Banff you will pass Castle Mountain - a glorious hunk of limestone, dolomite, and shale which, as its name suggests, looms over the Bow River like a mediaeval fortress. Popular with climbers, Castle Mountain rises to a height of 2766 metres above sea level.

The name 'Castle Mountain' dates to 1858 and is the title in use today. However, between 1946 and 1979, it had a different appellation: Eisenhower Mountain. The change came on orders from Prime Minister William Lyon Mackenzie King who wanted to honour Dwight D. Eisenhower, the supreme allied commander on the western front in World War II, when he visited Canada just after the return of peace. However, this caused considerable resentment because it replaced a long-standing and popular title and because people felt uncomfortable naming a mountain after a living person. Today Eisenhower's name is associated only with the separate 2752-metre tower at the east side of the main massif.

If you are an experienced rock climber, then you can scale the mountain. If you're not, there is a moderate 7.2-kilometre hike up to the base of the sheer walls for a splendid view of the surrounding countryside.

This trail departs from the Bow Valley Parkway, about five kilometres above Castle Mountain Junction on the road to Lake Louise.

In the past, Canadians were described romantically as 'hewers of wood and drawers of water' because so much of the economy was based on natural resources. Despite the country's 20th-century diversification into manufacturing, service industries, and other endeavours, primary resources continue to form the cornerstone of the nation's prosperity. Although extractive industries largely have disappeared from the national parks in the Rockies, traces of their former operations survive. Here, near Castle Mountain, there once was a boom town called Silver City. It was founded in 1883 to serve the needs of the CPR when the railway reached this spot. Shortly after, rumours of silver in the area precipitated an influx of prospectors so that the population quickly reached 2000. Within two years, the railway had moved on, the promise of silver had proved to be false, and Silver City lay deserted. Deserted, that is, except for one old coot, Joe Wilson, who hunted and trapped in the area until the 1930s. The Silver City site is in a meadow near the Bow River Parkway.

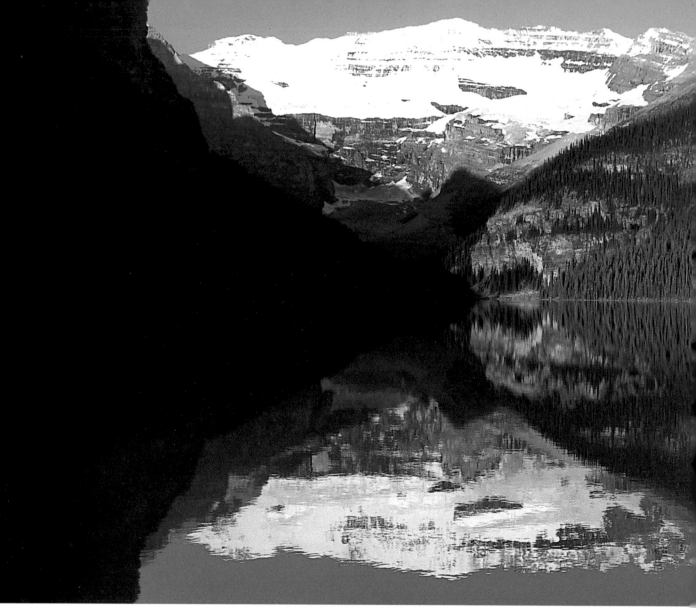

Lake Louise in its summer brilliance.

LAKE LOUISE AND VICTORIA GLACIER

About 55 kilometres northwest of the town of Banff is one of Canada's most famous natural attractions: Lake Louise. The deep green lake, surrounded by mountains and glaciers, has drawn sightseers for over a century who have marvelled at the natural beauty and have wondered why the lake is such a strong, almost shocking green colour. It comes from sunlight hitting the lake's floating mineral deposits of 'rock flour' which come suspended in the meltwaters from Victoria Glacier.

Lake Louise is the daughter of Victoria Glacier. In the distant past, the glacier covered the whole lake. It gradually deposited debris to form a landscape feature called a 'terminal moraine' which acted as a dam

to hold meltwater as the glacier slowly retreated. Today the lake, created by the moraine and sitting at an elevation of 1731 metres, is 2.4 kilometres long, 500 metres wide, and 90 metres deep. Native peoples called it 'the Lake of Little Fishes.' Its modern name honours Princess Louise Caroline Alberta, a daughter of Queen Victoria who married the Marquis of Lorne. The marquis served as Canada's governor-general from 1878 to 1883 during that great age of westward expansion when the lake became prominent after the Canadian Pacific Railway reached it in 1883.

In 1890, a wood chalet opened to serve the needs of Victorian tourists. The building burned in 1893, but was succeeded by a new guest house which could accom-

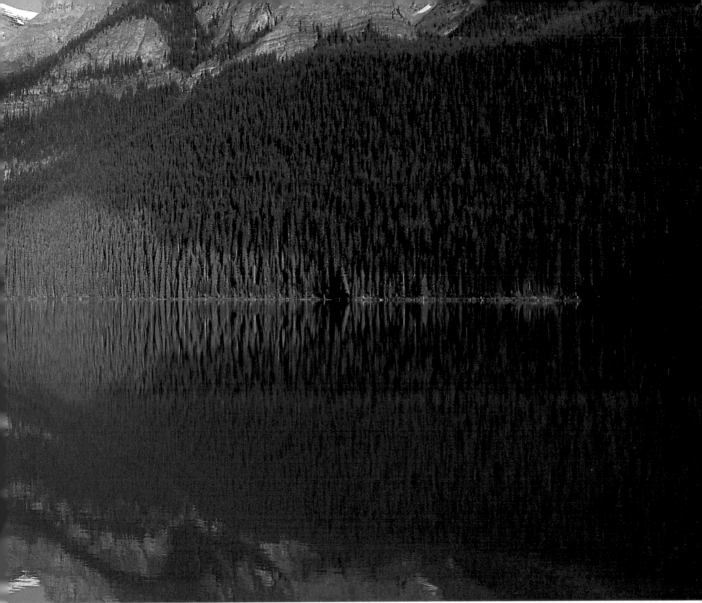

Under Victoria Glacier at the water's edge.

Following pages: the Lake Louise panorama with the Chateau Lake Louise in the foreground, as seen from the local gondola ride.

modate 12 travellers. Gradually, the CPR replaced, then enlarged the guest house so that by 1913 the Tudoresque Chateau Lake Louise could sleep 400 tourists. Rising more than 3460 metres above sea level behind Lake Louise is Mount Victoria. First conquered in 1897, it became a favourite target for the 'alpiners' who came to the Rockies in quest of a successful climbing holiday. The people behind the conquest of 1897 brought along a Swiss mountaineer by the name of Peter Sarbach to help ensure success. Sarbach's work inspired the CPR to hire a number of Swiss guides in 1899 to help attract tourists to Lake Louise. These people became a fixture at the lake until mountain guiding died out in the 1950s.

A boathouse where you can rent a canoe. Below: peaceful explorations.

Lake Louise and Victoria Glacier, views to capture the imagination.

Beyond its visual and mountaineering pleasures, Lake Louise is the centre of Canada's largest ski area, kept in prime condition by an average winter's snowfall of 4.2 metres. Lake Louise is also a good starting point for hikers seeking out the remote high country along the Continental Divide. Even if you're not a hiker, you will enjoy a walk along the Lake Louise shore line. If you want more exercise, then set off on some of the 70 kilometres of marked hiking trails which offer countless breathtaking panoramas for your pleasure. One particularly popular hike is the Plain of Six Glaciers Trail to a stunning lookout over Victoria Glacier and Lake Louise. If you get hungry en route, there is a tearoom (open during the summer) about five kilometres from the chateau. If you don't want to walk or ski, you can hire a canoe, a boat, or a horse to survey Lake Louise and its environs for a few hours or a day. If you have the time, you can mount a horse for a guided trail ride, lasting anywhere from three days to two weeks. Another excursion is the Lake Louise Gondola Lift to take you up over 2000 metres to Mount Whitehorn where views stretch over Lake Louise and across to the Valley of the Ten Peaks and the Bow Valley.

Many people think Lake Louise is even more delightful in winter, and find pleasure skating on the lake's cold weather ice rink. This page: the artistry of ice sculptures and the thrill of downhill skiing.

Mount Victoria and its dramatic glacier.

CHATEAU LAKE LOUISE

Today's Chateau Lake Louise, capable of housing 1000 guests, is one of Canadian Pacific's most famous hotels and one of North America's best loved places to stay. Like its famous cousin, the Banff Springs Hotel, the chateau had its founding in the late 19th century as a destination for travellers who took the CPR west from Toronto, Montreal, and other population centres in central Canada as well as from the United States and abroad. Ever on the lookout to improve the tourist trade, the railway added such creature comforts to the hotel as electricity in 1916-17 and a narrow-gauge tram to move people from the old railway station to the hotel (and which ran between 1912 and 1930). The chateau is one spot where you will want to blow your budget and luxuriate in its warmth. However, as almost every other visitor to the Rockies with a bit of extra cash wants to do the same thing, you need to make reservations months in advance if you plan to stay during the summer or winter high seasons. Recently remodelled, the chateau offers year-round comforts, restaurants, a spa, shopping, and various forms of entertainment to keep you happy. Even if you don't spend the night at the hotel, you should visit to enjoy its charming gardens, savour its public rooms, and have tea, a meal, or indulge in another of the chateau's services.

Summer and winter in and about the popular Chateau Lake Louise.

OLD RAIL STATION
AND POST HOTEL

The old log railway station at Lake Louise served travellers for about a century until train service to the village came to a halt in the 1980s. Now, this handsome historic building from a bygone era has become a bar and restaurant. Its old waiting room accommodates both pizza and fine dining, while the former ticketing lobby is the place to retreat for a quiet drink. Outside, on the track, are two vintage railway dining cars where you can relish excellent grilled meats.

Begun in 1942 as a humble ski lodge, the Post Hotel was completely remodelled by new European owners between 1988 and 1993 to become one of the more luxurious places to stay in the Rockies. Built in traditional log and beam construction, the hotel boasts charming public rooms, a renowned restaurant, a two-storey wood-panelled library, and gorgeous views of the peaks over Lake Louise and Moraine Lake.

Always known for superb dining, the revitalized Post Hotel has built on that tradition and now offers some of the finest food in the Rockies. A bit pricey, but worth the cost, this is the place to eat full-flavoured meats and fish such as salmon in a champagne and passion fruit sauce.

While you savour the comfort of the Post Hotel, you can reflect on how far we've come since the first tourist visited Lake Louise. He was A.P. Coleman, a geology professor from Toronto, who arrived in 1884. Professor Coleman paid 50 cents to share a bed with some smelly drunk in a log shack for the night! (The next day, he found another place to stay.)

The Old Rail Station and Post Hotel below Lake Louise.

Overlooking the Wenkchemna Valley.

WENKCHEMNA PEAKS (VALLEY OF THE 10 PEAKS)

Wenkchemna is the word for 'ten' in the language of the Stoney people. One of the largest mountains in the Rockies, Mount Temple, sits here, towering over the northwest edge of the Wenkchemna Valley. Its girth consumes 15 square kilometres of the Rockies topography, and, at 3350 metres, it is the third tallest mountain in Banff National Park.

The Wenkchemna Peaks are a good example of the scenic majesty that Victorian Canadians wanted to protect when they established national parks, starting with Banff in 1885. Originally, the federal government, Canadian Pacific Railway officials, and other interested people saw the need to set aside land that never could be acquired by private concerns (although the CPR seems to have played a particularly strong role in ensuring that development fulfilled its corporate interests).

Between 1885 and 1887, the government created six mountain reserves that form the nuclei of today's Banff, Yoho, Kootenay, Glacier, Mount Revelstoke, and Waterton Lakes national parks. To a large degree, these initiatives were possible back then because much of western Canada consisted of federally-owned undeveloped territory. By the early 20th century, the government began to establish parks elsewhere in the country, and gradually created na-

tional parks in most of Canada's distinct ecological regions. To protect the parks for all time, activities that might degrade these natural areas, such as mining, forestry, and hunting, either are forbidden or are controlled carefully. Mining licences, for example, have not been issued in the parks since 1930 and the last mining enterprise, at Yoho, ceased operations in 1952. Nevertheless, in some areas of heavy tourist traffic, such as Banff, there has been acrimonious debate in recent years between the advocates and opponents of development over how much growth or environmental compromise is acceptable.

Most visitors experience the national parks within or near the towns and roadways. Most of the parks' land mass, however, sits in the back country. There, you will encounter few tourists and have superb opportunities to trek along high river valleys, through alpine meadows, and march up close to frigid icefields. You can strike out on your own into the wilderness if you wish, but you need to obtain a permit from the park authorities first. At the same time you get your permit, you can pick up the necessary topographical maps, guides, and brochures. Be sure to read the pamphlet about what to do if you encounter a bear! (Climbing up a tree isn't a good idea; most bears climb better than us.)

Canoeing is a relaxing way to enjoy Moraine Lake near Lake Louise.

Following pages: the Wenkchemna Peaks behind Moraine Lake.

MORAINE LAKE

Less than 15 kilometres from Lake Louise is Moraine Lake in the Valley of the Wenkchemna Mountains. Many visitors, to their surprise, feel that it is even more exquisite and spectacular than its larger and more famous cousin. Therefore, be sure to make the trip! Here, you will marvel at the unforgettable sight of the glacial lake framed by the dramatic Wenkchemna Peaks soaring up towards the heavens.

The lake is misnamed! The person who christened it in 1899, Walter Wilcox, thought it, like Lake Louise, had its origins because of a terminal glacial moraine. (A moraine is a kind of dam created by the debris left behind by a glacier which blocks up a valley so that a lake can form behind it.) However, this lake formed after a rock fall from its neighbour, the 'Tower of Babel,' dammed the run-off from the surrounding mountains to create Moraine Lake. You can explore the story of the lake's formation along a short interpretive trail to the top of the tower's rock and debris hill. After hiking along this or one of the other local trails, you might want to retreat to the Moraine Lake Lodge on the lake shore to relax and enjoy a meal. Other nearby facilities include a good picnic area, interpretive exhibits, canoe rentals, and tourist accommodation.

CROWFOOT GLACIER

One of the leading attractions along the Icefields Parkway is the Crowfoot Glacier. It got its name because it resembled a huge three-toed claw - a crow's foot - when discovered a century or so ago. Today, the name seems a bit inappropriate because the glacier has retreated since the 1870s and one of the 'toes' broke off in the 1940s. Thus, it now resembles a two-pronged wishbone, but it nevertheless remains one of the most popular of the 100 or so glaciers along the parkway.

For years travel between Banff and Jasper was difficult, if not nearly impossible. Then, in the 1930s, construction began on the Banff-Jasper Highway as a make-work project during the Depression. The gravel road opened for automobile traffic in 1940. As tourism and traffic grew, this route, with its twists and turns, proved inadequate to meet changing demands. In the early 1960s, the new Icefields Parkway, placed largely on top of the old road, replaced the Banff-Jasper Highway and today is one of the most spellbinding routes motorists can take.

BOW LAKE

When the Icefields Parkway (also known as Highway 93) leaves Lake Louise, it proceeds north along the Bow River. At the headwaters of the river sits Bow Lake, one of the larger glacial lakes you will encounter along the road. It is fed by the Bow Glacier at the top of the valley which itself is connected to the Wapta Icefield farther west. At the lake, you can see the Bow Glacier which serves as one of five outlets for the 40-square-kilometre icefield.

Trout fishing is popular at the south end of the lake. Moose can be seen at the lake's swampier parts. Moose are the largest animals with antlers in the world, with adult male moose typically standing two metres tall at the shoulder. They like Bow Lake and the roadsides along the parkway, so chances are good that you will see one en route from Banff to Jasper. It looks like a great clumsy creature, but a moose can manage dense bush with ease, conquer deep snows, swim well, and, if it wants, run at speeds that exceed 50 kilometres per hour! Even though they are vegetarians, stay inside your car if you meet one; otherwise, you might meet your doom, especially if you disturb a female protecting its calf, or if you bother them during rutting season.

Two views of Crowfoot Glacier. Below: glacially-fed Bow Lake.

Num-ti-jah Lodge on Bow Lake. Num-ti-jah is an aboriginal word for the local marten, a member of the weasel family.

Following pages: Peyto Lake as seen from the Bow Summit Trail, 300 metres above the valley floor.

NUM-TI-JAH LODGE

Jimmy Simpson, an early outfitter and guide, built Num-ti-jah Lodge beside Bow Lake in 1920 when the region still was isolated wilderness. It replaced a more primitive camp that he and his wife, Billie, had operated on the spot for the previous two decades. Simpson arrived in the region in 1899 and became famous for his ability to find big game to satisfy the rich American hunters who holidayed at the camp. He died in 1972 at the age of 95; and in 1974 had a mountain named after him.

PEYTO LAKE

Before descending into the North Saskatchewan River drainage region along the Icefields Parkway, you will encounter Peyto Lake, celebrated for its natural beauty and turquoise water. The lake got its name from a famous guide and park warden, Ebenezer William (or 'Wild Bill') Peyto. He came to the Rockies in the 1890s and remained until his death in 1943. Like many of the early outfitters, this Englishman was renowned for his individualism as well as his fondness for fringed buckskins and the other clichés of western garb, complete with a six-shooter on his hip.

A view of Mount Chephren.
Opposite: upper: in the North Saskatchewan River Valley;
lower: a classic western building at the Crossing.

MOUNT CHEPHREN

Mount Chephren, at 3307 metres, lies behind Chephren Lake, west of the Waterfowl lakes beside the Icefields Parkway. Considered one of the finest mountains in the Rockies from an aesthetic perspective, it is visible for much of the parkway between Bow Pass and Big Bend Hill. Originally named Pyramid Mountain, its name was changed to Mount Chephren in 1918 to avoid confusion with another mountain with the same name in Jasper. Nevertheless, the new title kept alive the link to its earlier one because it is named after the son and successor of Cheops, the builder of Egypt's Great Pyramid.

You can get close to Mount and Lake Chephren along the Chephren Lake Trail which runs west from a point 1.2 kilometres south of the Waterfowl Lake Campground. The trail takes you four kilometres to Lake Chephren along swampy meadows and dense forest. At about the halfway point of the trail, if you have the energy, you can take another hike, this time along the Cirque Lake Trail which, at 10 kilometres, leads to a beautiful subalpine lake with superb fishing opportunities. These trails are just two of a large number of accessible hiking opportunities you will find along the Icefields Parkway.

SASKATCHEWAN RIVER CROSSING

In the old days, one of the more trying challenges facing people in the Rockies was the North Saskatchewan River, a difficult waterway to cross, particularly at high water. The result: many small and large tragedies occurred as people and horses attempted to pass through it. ('Saskatchewan' comes from the Cree language, and means 'swift current.') Even in the 1930s, bridging the river for the Banff-Jasper Highway proved to be an unusually demanding and exhausting project. Today, as motorists whiz across the bridge, it is almost impossible to imagine how different things were back then. Although the river itself proved to be a problem, the climate in the area is warmer and drier than elsewhere in the Rockies. With its higher temperatures and lighter snowfalls, this region is a magnet for deer, bighorn sheep, and mountain goats which also, of course, makes it an excellent place for nature lovers who want to see these wild creatures.

The 285-kilometre Icefields Parkway does not have many facilities for tourists, although there are a number of simple hotels for hikers and cyclists. (Cyclists usually take two or three days to travel the parkway.) However, the Saskatchewan River Crossing, about 153 kilometres south of Jasper, offers travellers accommodation, food, gas, souvenirs, and other services.

MISTAYA CANYON

If you are in a hurry, you can drive the Icefields Parkway in three or four hours. But if you do, you will miss all the great things to see along the way, such as the Mistaya Canyon. Situated a few kilometres south of the Saskatchewan River Crossing, it is one of the prettiest canyons in the west. It was created over many centuries because the Mistaya River carved its way through the local limestone to form the valley. The river, like so many in the region, starts off in a glacier above Peyto Lake. The word, 'Mistaya' by the way, is a Stoney expression for 'much wind.'

At the canyon, you can enjoy a 1.5-kilometre trail, easy enough for a family to traverse in an hour. The footpath starts off on an old road. Here, you will pass through a subalpine forest to the very narrow canyon. At the canyon, you can admire the sight of the Mistaya River as it plunges over the canyon walls on its way to the North Saskatchewan River. The latter river is 1216 kilometres long. Over 80 percent of its volume comes from the Rockies as meltwater.

The dramatic Mistaya Canyon near the Icefields Parkway.

GLACIER NATIONAL PARK

Located along the Trans-Canada Highway, Glacier National Park in British Columbia is home to over 400 glaciers amidst the Columbia Mountains, a mountain range situated west of the Rockies. The park occupies 1345 square kilometres of wild land which incorporates some of the tallest peaks in the Columbias. This range is older than the Rockies, composed of much harder rock which means that erosion takes place at a significantly slower pace. Thus, the range consists of steep, sharp mountains which hover over narrow valleys below.

The primary attractions at Glacier are the opportunities to hike along craggy peaks and enjoy the distinct life zones: interior rain forest, sub-alpine forest, alpine forest, tundra, and glacier-encrusted mountain tops.

Because of their location, the Columbias receive vast amounts of moist air from the Pacific Ocean to the west. As the air rises to meet the mountains, it cools quickly. Consequently, immense quantities of persistent rain and snow fall within a relatively mild climate compared to the Rockies. The park is the home of the famous Rogers Pass. Back in the 1880s, a major problem for the Canadian Pacific Railway was the challenge of breaching the Columbias to build Canada's critical rail link to the Pacific Ocean. The Rogers Pass, discovered in 1881, seemed to offer the solution. Sadly, the steep grades and local avalanche conditions posed a never-ending threat to humans and their endeavours. Finally, the completion of the eight-kilometre Connaught Tunnel under Mount Macdonald in 1916 shortened the route west and avoided the perils of the pass. Another railway tunnel replaced this one in 1988. At 14.4 kilometres, this new Mount Macdonald Tunnel is the longest in North America.

Commemorative monument to the Rogers Pass.

YOHO NATIONAL PARK

'Yoho' is a Cree word meaning 'awe.' It is a fitting name for this 1313-square-kilometre park with its many amazing sights. Located in British Columbia, between Glacier and Banff national parks, one of Yoho's attractions is the Natural Bridge, located 1.5 kilometres off the Trans-Canada near the village of Field.

The Kicking Horse River here encounters a strong formation of limestone rock.

The river cut a hole in the rock over the centuries to create a bridge which allows water to flow through a narrow slit.

Another fascinating feature in Yoho is the Burgess Shale Deposit with an extremely important collection of rare fossils from the Middle Cambrian period of 530 million years ago. Declared a World Heritage Site by UNESCO, you can visit the deposit on a tour led by a licensed guide.

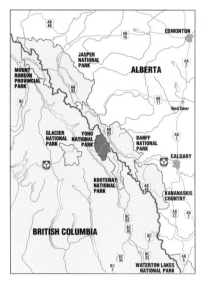

TAKAKKAW FALLS

Situated in some of the most scenic parts of Yoho, at the end of a narrow and winding road, is the Takakkaw Falls, Canada's second highest waterfall at 380 metres. You can enjoy the falls from the road which runs through the Yoho Valley, but a more exciting view is yours to behold if you hike along an easy path to the picnic area beside the falls. (The word 'Takakkaw' comes from the Stoney native expression 'it is wonderful.') From the falls, hikers can march off on a number of excellent trails to explore the upper subalpine and alpine ecoregions of the Yoho Valley, examine glaciers, and otherwise savour the wonderful range of local ecosystems. For those who want to spend several days in the wilderness, the park maintains a number of primitive, back country campsites to meet their needs.

The Natural Bridge in Yoho.

Following pages: the rugged beauty of Takakkaw Falls, 380 metres high.

Enjoying Emerald Lake in the Yoho Valley.

Winter and summer at the lake's tea house.

EMERALD LAKE

Truly beautiful Emerald Lake, Yoho's largest, is located close to Field. Like many of its brothers and sisters in the Rockies, it was formed 11,000 years ago by the damming effect of an old glacial moraine. The moraine is located where the Emerald Lake Lodge, first built in 1902, now sits.

Perhaps the best way to enjoy the lake is to take a walk along a pretty five-kilometre trail around its perimeter. Fishing, canoeing, cycling, skiing, and riding are other popular pursuits in and around the lake. This favourite site, like Takakkaw Falls and some of Yoho's other attractions, offers 'barrier free' access to at least some of its natural wonders for people in wheelchairs.

Lake O'Hara, positioned directly across the Continental Divide from Lake Louise, is another acclaimed destination in Yoho. With its diverse ecosystems and dazzling mountain views, the Lake O'Hara region draws visitors who want to explore its 80 kilometres of hiking trails. The lake is easily accessible by bus which serves its campground and lodge. However, efforts to preserve the ecosystem mean that the access road is not open to private vehicles and you have to make reservations about a month in advance if you want to stay overnight or even ride the bus into the region.

KOOTENAY NATIONAL PARK

RADIUM HOT SPRINGS

Located in British Columbia, south of Yoho, 1406-square-kilometre Kootenay National Park encompasses two river valleys, the Kootenay and Vermilion, amidst the stunning environment of the west side of the Rocky Mountains.

The Radium Hot Springs serve as the park's major tourist destination. Situated in a picturesque setting below the cliffs of Sinclair Canyon, they consist of two outdoor pools. One is kept at a hot 40 degrees Celsius for your relaxation; the other is a cooler swimming pool at a comfortable 29 degrees.

Unlike other hot springs in the Rockies, the ones here are virtually odourless and possess only a small mineral content; although, like the name suggests, they do contain a tiny, but safe, amount of radium.

SINCLAIR CANYON

You can see the kind of faulting that supplies the hot springs at the Redwall Fault close to the springs. This fault forms the Sinclair Canyon with its dramatic, vertical cliffs. The canyon itself at the west end of the park was created thousands of years ago through water erosion. You can tell this because of its 'V shape,' in contrast to glacially-carved 'U-shaped' valleys with flatter bottoms. Water-eroded valleys are less common than glacier valleys in the mountains because most either were formed by glaciers, or were started via water erosion but finished, by glacial action. Kootenay National Park itself dates to 1920 at the time when the automobile began to replace the train as the main vehicle tourists would use to enjoy their holidays: 4500 Model T's and other vehicles visited the park that first year!

Relaxing at Radium Hot Springs.

A dramatic view of Sinclair Canyon.

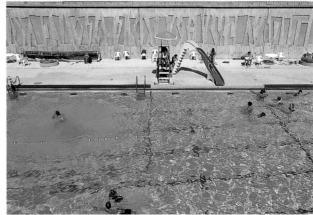

The Kootenay River Valley, a sublime place to escape, breathe fresh air, and unwind.

KOOTENAY RIVER

The Kootenay River Valley serves local wildlife as a transportation corridor and hence provides excellent opportunities to see mule and white-tailed deer, elk, black bear, coyotes, moose, and wolves. As well as 250 species of animals, Kootenay presents visitors with a tremendous range of natural diversity within four distinct mountain topographies, with almost 1000 different plants finding a habitat in the park.

The word 'Kootenay' is the name the local natives applied to themselves and means 'river people.' According to ancient pictographs found nearby, the plains and the mountain peoples probably met regularly at Kootenay's hot springs. The water in these springs, like those found elsewhere in the Rocky Mountains, starts as run-off from the earth's surface, but drains down at least 2415 metres into the ground. There, near the hot inner regions of the planet, it is heated to 100 degrees and turns into steam, then rises through faults again, condensing en route, to emerge at the surface at between 32 and 54 degrees Celsius.

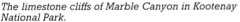
The limestone cliffs of Marble Canyon in Kootenay National Park.

MARBLE CANYON

Towards the north end of Kootenay National Park, 90 kilometres from Radium, is Marble Canyon, one of the most colourful canyons in the park with its myriad plants, 36-metre cliffs, and blue glacial meltwater. There is a short 0.8-kilometre trail to follow which passes through the more scenic areas, dramatically crosses Tokumm Creek, and ends at a striking waterfall. (Tokumm comes from the Stoney language and means 'red fox.') Along the way you will encounter various kinds of vegetation, including plants normally seen only in arctic environments because of the cool and damp air that dominates the canyon.

A few kilometres south of Marble Canyon is the Paint Pots Trail, a paved 1.5-kilometre pathway which passes through a lower subalpine forest and across a long, low bridge over the Vermilion River before climaxing at the Ochre Beds and Paint Pots. Here, cold springs push iron-rich water to the surface. In ancient days, the Kootenay people gathered up the red clay and made it into body paint which they used themselves and which they traded to the Stoney tribe. Another attraction, about seven kilometres to the northwest of the Marble Canyon, is the Vermilion Pass Burn. In 1968, fire destroyed 2400 hectares of forest. Today, the site of this conflagration is a wonderful place to go and see how an area regenerates itself as part of the natural process from new to mature forest, to fire, to rebirth.

KANANASKIS COUNTRY

THREE SISTERS

The Three Sisters Mountains sit southeast of Canmore in the Kananaskis Country of Alberta near the Trans-Canada Highway. For many people, these peaks are the hallmark of the 4000-square-kilometre Kananaskis region. This area comprises the often-overlooked front ranges of the Rocky Mountains situated west of Calgary and south of Banff. It is home of several ecological zones, including rolling foothills to the east, a higher montane region, alpine meadows, and farther west, an alpine zone at elevations of 1830 to 2440 metres, complete with glaciers along the Continental Divide. An added attraction is the weather: it generally is warmer and sunnier here than in the more famous national parks. As well, crowds tend to be smaller than in Banff and Jasper.

Originally home of the Stoney and Sarcee tribes, the lower elevations were settled in the late 19th and early 20th centuries by people who wanted to exploit the ranching, forestry, mining, and hydro-electric opportunities available to them. Most of the region today is devoted to nature conservation and recreational uses, particularly in the area's provincial parks. With fewer restrictions on development compared to the national parks, leisure facilities are particularly well-developed in Kananaskis.

For western enthusiasts, this is the place to go for ranching vacations and trail rides. Skiing is popular here as well, as are golfing, hiking, mountain climbing, horseback riding, fishing, camping, and a wide variety of other winter and summer sports.

Mount Kidd near the recreational centre of Kananaskis Village.

The Three Sisters near Canmore.

Mount Assiniboine's peak. This page: skiing in Kananaskis Country.

MOUNT ASSINIBOINE

At 3618 metres, Mount Assiniboine's peak - the 'Matterhorn of the Rockies' - dominates the British Columbia provincial park by the same name just over the border from Alberta's Kananaskis Country. Established in 1922, the park serves the interests of nature lovers, hikers, climbers, horseback riders, and cross-country skiers. There is a lodge along with some cabins in the park at Lake Magog; although, in contrast to Kananaskis Country, facilities are few and primitive, thus appealing to alpine purists. The park is closed to vehicles, so most people backpack their way in to enjoy its pristine scenery while others fly in via helicopter.

Back in Alberta, however, the Kananaskis Country's excellent slopes were used for the skiing events at the 1988 Calgary Winter Olympics. The Nordic Centre in the town of Canmore is a legacy from the Olympics, maintained for the benefit of cross-country skiing enthusiasts. Downhill skiing fans will want to travel a bit south to the Olympic slopes of Nakiska. The region now provides every conceivable skiing opportunity, from family-oriented cross-country skiing, to Olympic-quality downhill, to wild (and dangerous) heliskiing, and more.

TRANS-CANADA HIGHWAY

While Canada had a transcontinental railway from the 1880s, a single road linking the country from the Atlantic to the Pacific did not become a reality until completion of the Trans-Canada Highway in 1962. Formally opened at the Rogers Pass, this 7821-kilometre route crosses the provinces to link east with west. Today, it is the world's longest national highway, although, in the Rockies, it does have difficulty keeping up with summertime tourist traffic because the volume of visitors has expanded so rapidly in recent years.

If your visit to the Canadian Rockies were to start in Calgary, you would drive west along the Trans-Canada through prairie, then foothills, until you reached Canmore and the mountains before continuing on to Banff. From there, you could drive north to Lake Louise where the Icefields Parkway carries on north to Jasper. The Trans-Canada, on the other hand, turns west after Lake Louise, crossing over the Continental Divide from Banff into Yoho National Park. From there it proceeds west to Golden, British Columbia and on to Glacier and Mount Revelstoke national parks before continuing its long journey to the Pacific Ocean.

Back on the east side of the Rockies, the town of Canmore is the main community in the Kananaskis region. Formerly a coal-mining centre, it now serves as a bedroom community for Calgary and Banff as well as the hub of Kananaskis Country's travel-trade industry. Its attractions include various tourism facilities, a museum, a restored historic Northwest Mounted Police barracks, as well as a number of commercial art galleries and craft shops. Canmore also hosts annual summer festivals for both Albertans and visitors to the province. Another local tourism centre is Kananaskis Village, on Highway 40 which runs south from the Trans-Canada to Peter Lougheed Provincial Park, where you can partake in excellent golf, winter skiing, and other recreational diversions.

Moody weather along the Trans-Canada Highway.

JASPER NATIONAL PARK

COLUMBIA ICEFIELD

The dramatic Columbia Icefield near the Icefields Parkway is an interlocking system of glaciers which cover 390-square-kilometres of land. At some points, the ice is a staggering 365 metres thick! That the icefield is the remnant of the ancient ones that covered most of Canada during the ice age of thousands of years ago is another cause of amazement. Therefore, the Columbia Icefield is not to be missed. Located 125 kilometres north of Lake Louise (or 105 kilometres south of the Jasper town site) the icefield also is known as the mother of rivers because its meltwaters feed the Fraser, Athabasca, Columbia, and Saskatchewan river systems. Of the 30 glaciers in the field, the largest are the Saskatchewan and Athabasca glaciers. You can see the Athabasca, Stutfield, and Dome glaciers from the parkway. Glaciers are formed by the compaction and recrystallization of snow into ice crystals. They usually also incorporate air, water, and rock debris. The glacial field advances and contracts: the last advance occurred about the year 1840. Each year, an average snowfall of 10 metres helps renew the glacial resource.

You can visit the Athabasca Glacier on a special 'Snowcoach,' a large, specially designed bus that takes you right out onto the ice. Once here, you can wander around and peer into one of the glacier's 30,000 crevasses, some of which are 30 metres deep. Alternatively, you can take a hike out onto the glacier so long as you go with a licensed guide. If you hear noises which sound like thunder while you're out here, they most likely come from avalanches farther up the glacier. Today, the glacier is over five kilometres long from its toe near the parkway back to the Columbia Icefield. It is about one kilometre broad at its widest.

A marker showing how far the Athabasca Glacier extended in 1908. It has shrunk 1.7 kilometres since 1870.

The Icefields Centre where you catch the snowcoach to the glacier and enjoy dioramas and other exhibits about the Columbia Icefield.

Following pages: upper: Athabasca Glacier; below: vintage and modern snowcoaches.

A 12-kilometre hike, accessible from the Wilcox Pass Campgrounds, provides the best views to be had of the Athabasca Glacier if you're game enough for the walk around the ice sheet's perimeter. You also may walk right up beside the glacier's 15-metre-thick toe. Standing here, you will see meltwater wherever you look. Some of that water took 150 years to travel from the top of the Athabasca Glacier, and some of it may have formed as long as 800 years ago. Because the water is full of sediments, however, you probably will want to forgo the chance to have a historic drink. Also, in summer, the local snow has a pink colour. The pink comes from algae which are eaten by tiny snow worms. Therefore, you probably won't want to dine on the snow either.

To complete your visit, make sure you go to the recently enlarged and wheelchair-accessible Icefield Centre. You will see displays, photographs, and films here to help you understand this truly magnificent part of the Canadian Rockies.

JASPER TOWN SITE

Jasper National Park, established in 1907, is named after Jasper Hawse, a local fur trader in the early 19th century. The centre of the park is the Jasper town site on the Athabasca River, 260 kilometres west of Edmonton. Tourists began to arrive here shortly after it became accessible via the Grand Trunk Pacific and Great Northern railways in 1911-12 and a town of sorts - composed of tents - began to grow. Facilities gradually improved, and in 1927, an all-weather road opened to Edmonton which further advanced Jasper's growth as a holiday destination.

Jasper today, at 10,880 square kilometres of glaciers, lakes, rivers, canyons, forests, alpine tundra, and mountains, is the largest of the Rocky Mountain parks. The place to start your tour is at the park's information building in the town where you can get the brochures, maps, and details you need to ensure you have a successful trip. The town offers the normal amenities of a Rocky Mountain tourist centre, including commercial art galleries and craft shops as well as all sorts of places to eat. The town also hosts a round of seasonal festivals and is home for two small museums, the Jasper Yellowhead Museum and the Den Wildlife Museum. It is quieter than Banff with a somewhat humbler feel and without the traffic jams

and line-ups that sometimes make its southern cousin frustrating. The town is an excellent place to use as a base for visiting other attractions in the region. If, for example, you did not get enough relaxation in the hot springs in Banff, then you probably will want to drive 60 kilometres northeast from town to the Miette Hot Springs where you can enjoy 40-degree Celsius water from the site's sulphur springs. One of the pools is wheelchair accessible. (The spring water actually has to be cooled down a bit to get it to a bearable 40 degrees from the 57 degrees as it comes out of the rocks.) Hiking trails abound in this park, including some easy ones near the town site. One, for example, is the wheelchair-accessible, 2.4-kilometre Annette Lake Loop. It consists of an asphalt path with interpretive signs and offers a number of pretty mountain vistas and a chance to go swimming or fishing in Lake Annette. You can even see some quicksand which, safely, is fenced off. Scuba divers like spring-fed Lake Annette because visibility is good at a distance of up to 30 metres below the water's surface. In winter, cross-country and downhill skiing are central to the life of Jasper, and one of the best downhill ski areas, with more than 50 runs, sits 12 kilometres west of Jasper.

Panorama of the Jasper town site in the Athabasca River Valley from Whistlers Mountain.

Jasper the Bear, the park mascot.

A hand-carved totem pole near the railway station.

Following pages: the superb view from the Tramway.

JASPER TRAMWAY

The Jasper Tramway is not a horizontal streetcar line as you might expect from its name. Rather, it is a glass-enclosed gondola to whisk you to the top of Whistlers Mountain at an altitude of 2277 metres. Each tramcar holds 30 passengers along with a guide who presents fascinating information about the surrounding region during the seven-minute ride. Alternatively, you can climb up an eight-kilometre trail if you think you're too tough for the tramway or if you want to examine the changing ecology up close.

Once you reach your destination, there is an interpretive centre to fill you in on the details of the alpine environment as well as a newly-renovated restaurant. The view of the Athabasca and Miette river valleys is glorious, and on clear days you can see as far as Canada's highest mountain, Mount Robson, 80 kilometres away in British Columbia. Located six kilometres south of the Jasper townsite along the Icefields Parkway, the tramway has sent almost five million people to the top of Whistlers since it opened. There

are boardwalk trails near the interpretive centre accessible for visitors in wheelchairs. A rougher trail reaches the peak of Whistlers Mountain. Along the way, you might see a hoary marmot, a big rodent that looks like a woodchuck, whose shrill whistle gave the peak its name. Don't forget to take a jacket: it can be cold up here, with snow, even in summer.

While you stare at all these massive mountains from your vantage point on top of Whistlers, it is almost natural to think that these are permanent, unchanging sentinels in the wild.

The reality, however, is otherwise. Every day they change slightly, and on some days dramatically, as evidenced by the ancient rock slides that are so abundantly clear in the Rockies. The small, everyday changes are harder to notice, but you will hear them if you listen carefully for the sound of a rock that has split off from its mountain to roll noisily down towards the nearest valley because of freeze-thaw or other factors.

In and about the Jasper Park Lodge, complete with a plains style teepee.

JASPER PARK LODGE

The Jasper Park Lodge on the shores of Lac Beauvert, seven kilometres east of the Jasper townsite, provides deluxe, year-round accommodation. The pretty lake itself, often visited by deer and elk, was created by melting glacial ice at the end of the last ice age. Lodge services include riding, tennis, golf, biking, boating, and fishing. Although the lodge boasts 442 units, and the rooms aren't cheap, you almost certainly will not find a vacancy during the peak seasons unless you book well in advance. Nevertheless, you can visit the lodge if you are not a guest to eat a fine dinner, to shop in one of its boutiques, or otherwise enjoy its amenities.

The lodge began operations in 1922 under the ownership of the Canadian National Railway, the successor to the Grand Trunk Pacific. Today Canadian Pacific Hotels runs it. Jasper Park Lodge originally consisted of a huge central log cabin where guests came to eat and socialize. They slept in smaller log cabins near the main building, a tradition that continues today. When you call room service from your cabin, the waiter delivers your order via bicycle. The golf course opened in 1925. The original main lodge burned in 1952 and the present-day structure is its replacement.

SUNWAPTA FALLS

The Stoney expression, 'Sunwapta' applied to the falls is well chosen because it means 'turbulent waters.' Here, the Sunwapta River changes its course sharply from northwest to southwest because its ancient route has been blocked up by a glacial moraine. Its waters now drop from the higher Sunwapta Valley into a deep limestone canyon before joining the Athabasca River. It is easily accessible from the Icefields Parkway, about 55 kilometres south of the Jasper town site.

There is an excellent four-kilometre trail which lets you appreciate a relatively unknown and much less crowded site near the upper Sunwapta Falls. It takes you through some scenic countryside to the lower Sunwapta Falls which, because of its relative isolation, is perhaps more exciting than the one most visitors see. You gain access to the trail near the upper falls and set off through the forest to the lower falls about two kilometres away. Like the upper waterfall, the lower one cascades through a tight breach in the rock. If you continue on for a few minutes more, you will encounter another pretty waterfall.

ATHABASCA FALLS

A popular destination 30 kilometres south of the Jasper town site on the Icefields Parkway is the Athabasca Falls. Here, the Athabasca River finds itself funnelled into a narrow canyon cut into the hard quartz sandstone. The result: the 25-metre Athabasca Waterfall is one of the most powerful in the Rockies. You can enjoy the falls along an interesting walkway, the Athabasca Falls Trail. It is a relaxing 1.4 kilometre hike that takes you past interpretive signs which explain the local geology as well as let you examine a now-defunct river channel where the waterfall was located at an earlier time. Some of the mountains you will see from this spot are Mounts Christie and Fryatt towards the south; Mount Kerkeslin to the southeast, and, to the west, Mount Edith Cavell. Kayakers are attracted to this area because there is an opportunity to start an exciting run towards Old Fort Point near the Jasper town site. Five or six kilometres away is another good hiking trail which will take you to Horseshoe Lake along a two-kilometre route. As in the Rockies as a whole, it is important to stay on the marked trails, both for your own safety and to prevent unnecessary damage to the fragile ecosystems.

Turbulent Sunwapta Falls.

Following pages: two imposing views of Athabasca Falls.

Majestic Mount Edith Cavell. This page: Angel Icefield and horses enjoying a cool drink at Cavell Glacier Lake.

MOUNT EDITH CAVELL

The majestic 3363-metre Mount Edith Cavell got its name in 1916 during the dark days of The First World War when Canadian troops fought in the trenches of western Europe alongside their British, French, and colonial compatriots.

Edith Louise Cavell was an English nurse who worked at a Belgian Red Cross hospital in Brussels. Accused by Belgium's German occupiers of helping allied prisoners escape, she was ordered shot for treason, a sentence that was carried out despite the efforts of the ambassador of the still-neutral United States to save her.

She was guilty under the military laws of the time and admitted her acts, but declared that she had assisted the prisoners in order to save their lives. She became a heroic symbol in Canada and elsewhere in the British Empire and so had the mountain named in her honour. Before 1916, it was known as 'La Montagne de la Grande Traverse' by Europeans in recognition of its role in pointing out an old fur trade route through the Rockies into British Columbia. Native people knew it as the 'White Ghost,' presumably in relation to the appearance of its snow-capped peak in moonlight.

The mountain, 20 kilometres south of the Jasper town site, is truly magnificent, and the Angel and Cavell glaciers and Cavell Glacier Lake near the mountain heightens the majesty of the scene. (The Angel Glacier originally looked like a spread-winged angel. However, the lower portions, the angel's dress, have disappeared since the 1920s so the logic behind the name has been lost.) A problem with getting to Mount Edith Cavell is that so many people want to see it that Cavell Road, opened in 1924, cannot meet the traffic flow. Therefore, during the busy summer season, the park authorities limit the amount of time you can spend here to an hour to prevent traffic jams and strains on the fragile environment.

PYRAMID MOUNTAIN

Some local people tell outsiders a joke by informing them, in a serious tone of voice, that Pyramid Mountain was built 2000 years ago by the ancient Egyptians. Pity the poor tourist who falls for that one! At 2766 metres, Pyramid Mountain dominates the local environment. If you look carefully at the summit, you will see a communications station up near the peak.

One of the questions visitors regularly ask when looking up the enormous slopes is: Why do the trees stop growing part way up the mountain? There are several reasons why you don't see trees above an average elevation of 2150 metres. One is the tiny amount of soil at higher elevations, caused because organic material decays at a snail's pace in the cold environment; so soil build-up is slow at the same time wind blows away most of what little accumulation occurs. Another is the very short growing season, usually only two months per year at the upper elevations. As well, it is cold up there. The average temperature on the mountain tops is minus four degrees Celsius, and frost can occur on any day of the year. Furthermore, snow hangs around until July which reduces the time for trees to grow a decent layer of protective bark to hold in the moisture they need to flourish. You can see the consequences in the old but stunted trees at the border between treed and treeless regions. But why, then, do so many pretty little flowering plants grow so high up? One reason is that, despite appearances, they are tough and adaptable, so they do well in the harsh conditions. They do not grow very tall, but they flourish during the short summer season. They also typically have wax-like or hairy leaves to retain moisture, and they often do not reproduce with seed, but do so via runners which is more efficient.

One way of enjoying Jasper is to take a guided hiking tour around Pyramid Mountain or through some other part of the park. Both the park staff and private companies offer guiding services to meet different interests. You can get lists of times, places, and prices at the information centre in the Jasper town site. When you book a tour, purchase a meal, or engage some other service while on vacation, you are making a contribution to the Canadian economy. Tourism is the nation's fifth-largest industry, generating about five percent of Canada's gross national product. In the Rockies, of course, tourism is even more important, being the main source of prosperity and employment.

Pyramid Mountain on clear and foggy days. Note the communications station on the top.
Below: the grandeur of Pyramid Mountain.

Two picturesque views of Pyramid Lake.

PYRAMID LAKE

Overlooking Pyramid Mountain, eight kilometres from the Jasper town site, Pyramid Lake is a glacial lake where you can fish or boat in its waters, or picnic, hike, or horseback ride around its shores. It also is one of only three lakes in all of the Rocky Mountain national parks where you can use a motor boat. Because of that, water skiing is popular here. As well, there are various lodges and other establishments to furnish you with everything you need to enjoy the lake's sporting opportunities. Favourite water sports at Pyramid Lake include canoeing, kayaking, pedal boating, and windsurfing. But, if you fall in the lake, you'll find the water to be rather chillier than you might wish it to be.

There is a little island in the lake, Pyramid Island, which you can visit by a footbridge. It is an enchanting spot with its trees, rustic shelter, and wonderful view across the lake to Pyramid Mountain. Bring your lunch for a memorable picnic. A good drive is to be had along the Patricia Lake/Pyramid Lake road where you can enjoy the rich montane forest, in both its dry and open wood format filled with wildlife, as well as through the damper environment of Cottonwood Slough, a montane wetland, filled with black spruce, and created by beaver damming activities. Cottonwood Slough is the place to see such birds as the rufus hummingbird, yellowthroat, northern waterthrush, and Wilson's warbler.

For the hiker, there is a seven-kilometre route, the Jasper-Pyramid Lake Trail, to take you through the same region. You begin the trail at the recreation centre in Jasper and enjoy excellent views of the surrounding mountains and Athabasca Valley en route. You even might encounter an elk, a moose, or a deer on the way, especially if you take this route in winter as a cross-country skiing enterprise. These animals find the lighter snows around here easier to dig through for the grass and plants they eat compared to the higher forest regions.

As you walk this and other trails, it is important to make as small an impact on the environment as possible. Do not pick the flowers: in many cases it is illegal. Also, don't litter: a cigarette butt, for example, can last up to five years as well as pose a fire hazard; glass bottles might lie around for a millennium, and your plastic film container might serve as a local eyesore for 30 years. And of course, hunting is not allowed in the Rocky Mountain national parks where some animals owe their survival to the sanctuary provided within these protected environments.

PATRICIA LAKE

Like Pyramid Lake, its neighbour Patricia Lake is fed by glaciers and offers recreational opportunities in a perfect natural setting. The 40-metre-deep lake is named after Lady Patricia Ramsay, one of Queen Victoria's granddaughters. At the lake, you can rent a canoe, and, if you have a permit, you can fish for rainbow trout. There is a good 4.8-kilometre hiking trail, the Patricia Lake Loop, which starts from the Pyramid Riding Stables, and takes you through jackpine, Douglas fir, and aspen woodlands to the lake above the Jasper town site.

Patricia Lake played a principal role in one of the more outlandish projects of the Second World War. After losing huge numbers of ships to enemy submarines in the Battle of the Atlantic, Canada and its allies experimented with new kinds of unsinkable shipping. One of the ideas, tested on Patricia Lake in 1943, was a vessel made out of ice and wood chips! The substance was called 'pikecrete' after its inventor, an Englishman named Geoffrey Pike. The idea was to build a kind of aircraft carrier/iceberg which would not sink if torpedoed and which would not melt in the cold North Atlantic. The experiment didn't work out. By the way, before coming to Canada to work on the project, Pike lived in a mental hospital.

Reflections on Patricia Lake.

ATHABASCA VALLEY

The Athabasca River is one of Canada's great waterways. Its historical importance was recognized in 1989 when the 168 kilometres of the river that runs through Jasper was designated a Canadian Heritage River. The waterway itself may be as old as the Rocky Mountains. It probably eroded down to its present level as the mountains were being lifted up, which accounts for its current course. The deep and wide valley in Jasper today is traversed by the Icefields and Yellowhead parkways.

The Yellowhead Pass in the Athabasca Valley connects Jasper to Mount Robson Provincial Park across the Continental Divide. The pass is the lowest in the Rockies. However, engineers in the 1880s found it too difficult for the Canadian Pacific Railway and abandoned it as a possible route through the Rockies in their drive to the west coast. About 30 years later, the Grand Trunk Pacific Railway (now Canadian National) cut its way through the pass.

The name 'Yellowhead' comes from a fair-haired Iroquois trapper, Pierre Hatsination, who lived in the region in the 1820s. The Iroquois are not indigenous to this area. However, hundreds of them from communities far to the east near Montreal came west in the late 18th and early 19th centuries to participate in the western fur trade.

The changing atmosphere of the Athabasca Valley.

MALIGNE CANYON

Primaeval rock, rushing white water, sheer limestone rock faces, and dramatic wilderness scenery combine to make Maligne Canyon a spectacular place to visit. The narrow canyon has been sculpted by water and frost to a depth of 55 metres over the last 10,000 years. Before then, the Maligne River dropped into the Athabasca River in a waterfall. However, the cutting force of the water, combined with the weakness of the rock, created today's valley. The current rate of erosion is one centimetre per annum as the Maligne River plunges through the steep walled gorge.

The canyon sits 11 kilometres from the Jasper town site. You can explore its fascinating landscape along self-guided, winding, interpretive trails which cross a number of foot bridges to provide particularly striking views. The canyon twists and turns so much because the water followed the path of least resistance and, therefore, used existing cracks and fissures to sculpt its way through the rock. At some places along the path, you will be surprised at how narrow the canyon can be, sometimes being little more than a metre wide. Because of the canyon's distinct cool, damp, and shaded microclimate, the rare birds and lush vegetation found here (along with intriguing fossils) make your visit more interesting.

Maligne Canyon, a product of 10,000 years of erosion.

White water thrills await visitors to the Rockies.

RAFTING

The wet and exhilarating world of white water rafting awaits the adventurous tourist in the Canadian Rockies, both in and outside of the national parks. Or, if you have a calmer soul, peaceful rafting tours are also offered throughout the region, such as a trip along the Bow River in Banff, an outing suitable for families with young children. Some companies have tours to provide enjoyable experiences for people with disabilities. To take the white water versions, however, you must be both fit and a strong swimmer. If you have the time, various outfitters arrange two-, three-, four-, and five-day rafting and canoe tours through beautiful and peaceful wilderness.

Usually the price you pay includes everything, from transportation to and from your hotel, to all the equipment you need, plus a trained guide, and meals. Some even offer gourmet food en route. You can find out about the various rafting services at the park information centres, or through reading advertisements in the commercial tourist magazines, or by checking out the details described in the provincial government's tourist literature.

MEDICINE LAKE

Medicine Lake sits between Maligne Lake and Maligne Canyon in Jasper National Park. It is a curious water feature because it has no surface outlets, but its water level fluctuates significantly over the course of a few months. The Maligne River, swollen in spring and summer with glacial run-off, feeds the lake so that the water level rises in summer and the six-kilometre lake looks quite charming. By autumn, the lake drains almost to the point of becoming a huge mud puddle. Local wits call it 'the leaky bathtub.'

Where does the water go? It drains downwards at the rate of 57 cubic metres per second into channels and caves carved out of the water-soluble limestone underneath the lake.

Most of it then reappears 16 or 17 kilometres downstream in the Maligne Canyon, and some of it seems to nourish the lakes near the Jasper town site. For most of the summer, the volume of water is too great for it all to drain quickly, so we have a very pretty lake during the warm months. When the backlog drains away by late autumn, it turns into a series of streams which criss-cross the mud flats.

When tourists think of the people who discovered Medicine Lake and other out-of-the-way Rocky Mountain sites in the late 19th and early 20th centuries, they typically assume that the early adventurers and mountain climbers were men. Aside from forgetting 50 percent of the aboriginal population, this assumption overlooks the women of European origins who found a home and excitement in the Canadian Rockies back in more primitive days. One of the more famous female explorers in Jasper was Mary Schäffer, a Quaker who originally hailed from Philadelphia. She came to the region in 1889 at the age of 28, and spent most of the rest of her life in the Rockies until her death in 1939. She was a noted early botanist, photographer, and writer whose efforts included publication of the popular Edwardian travel book, *Old Indian Trails of the Canadian Rockies.*

One of the more famous early female tourists to the Rocky Mountains was Lady Agnes Macdonald, wife of Canada's first prime minister, Sir John A. Macdonald. When the couple came west for a visit in the 1880s, Sir John looked at the scenery through the window of his luxurious private railway car. The more adventurous Lady Agnes enjoyed the view, for at least part of the way, from the vantage point of the 'cow catcher' on the front of the train. (One wonders if there was a holiday-centred domestic dispute behind all this - Sir John did tend to drink rather a lot in his day.)

This and following pages: pretty Medicine Lake in summer, before it drains to become a giant mud puddle in the autumn.

An Elk calls its friends. This page: the Maligne Lake Boathouse.

Following pages: Spirit Island, in Maligne Lake is one of the most photographed sights in the Rockies, for obvious reasons! It got its name from an early explorer, Mary Schäffer.

MALIGNE LAKE

Located 48 kilometres southeast of the Jasper town site, you won't want to miss this beautiful lake surrounded by subalpine forests. At 22 kilometres in length, one kilometre in width, and 96 metres deep, it is the largest (but not the deepest) lake in the Canadian Rockies. It also is the second largest glacier-fed lake in the world. Maligne Lake got its name from the river of the same name. For some uncertain reason, a Belgian Jesuit missionary, Pierre de Smet, gave the river the title in the 1840s. It is the French word for 'malignant' or 'wicked.' However, anyone looking at this beautiful lake can only wonder why it has such an unfortunate name.

Rather than ponder de Smet's motives, a better way to enjoy the waters is to take a 90-minute narrated boat cruise. (Because of demand, you should book your tour in advance at the Jasper town site.) Tour boats have cruised the lake since 1928. Alternatively, you can rent a boat or canoe at the Maligne Lake Boathouse to explore the lake under your own steam. If you want to fish, the boathouse can provide you with a fishing licence and tackle. Maybe you'll beat the Alberta record for catching a 9.3 kilogram rainbow trout! Brook trout also are common here.

If you don't know the best fishing spots, you can hire a professional guide to take you to his or her favourite spot among Jasper's 800 lakes and ponds. Guide fees usually include the boat, tackle, lunch, and rain gear. As usual with the Rockies, there are good hiking trails around Maligne Lake, one of which is the Skyline Trail, a demanding 44-kilometre route along the crest of the Maligne Range of mountains, suitable for the hard-core hiker.

One of the large animals in the Canadian Rockies which lives in the high regions around Jasper not far from Maligne Lake is the cougar. However, you probably won't see this rare and reclusive animal during your vacation. This cat, which can grow to a hefty 70 kilograms, hunts alone in search of various animals, its favourite being mule deer. Two other wild cats in the Rockies, also infrequently seen, are bobcats and lynx.

Feathered hunters which are more likely to appear while you are here are golden and bald eagles as well as ospreys. Eagles are the most frequently seen large birds in the region. These huge creatures with their two-metre wing span feed on fish, rabbits, rodents, and the dead animals they find. Bald eagles nest on tree tops while golden eagles prefer cliff edges. The osprey likes to hunt along lakes and rivers in the montane and lower subalpine regions. It is a bit smaller than an eagle, but no less a fearsome hunter in its search for smaller birds, rodents, and fish.

MOUNT ROBSON PROVINCIAL PARK

At 2170 square kilometres, Mount Robson Provincial Park sits inside British Columbia just west of Jasper National Park along the Yellowhead Highway. Founded in 1913, it is home to snow-capped mountains, deep canyons, icefields, lakes, and the upper reaches of the mighty Fraser River.

Standing majestically above all is the tallest mountain in the Canadian Rockies, Mount Robson at 3954 metres above sea level.

(The second tallest is Mount Columbia near the Columbia Glacier which is 200 metres shorter.) Mount Robson was known to the aboriginal peoples as 'the mountain of the spiral road' because its huge spiral ledges angle upwards towards the peak. As climbers have found out over the years, the ledges do not reach all the way to the summit. The route up is a particularly challenging climb. The first people known to have tried to conquer Mount Robson were Professor A.P. Coleman and the Reverend George Kinney in 1908.

They failed in their attempt, but Kinney tried again in 1909 with a British adventurer, L.S. Amery. They scaled the treacherous west face of the mountain and claimed to have succeeded, but today people think they turned back short of their goal. Nevertheless, nobody since has attacked the perilous west face. The first definite conquest occurred in 1911 when an Austrian mountain guide, Conrad Kain, reached the summit with two members of the Alpine Club of Canada, W.W. Foster and A.H. MacCarthy. Since then Mount Robson has attracted climbers from around the world, but reaching the peak is a rare event. Between 1939 and 1953, for example, nobody succeeded in vanquishing the mountain.

Mount Robson, the tallest peak in the Canadian Rockies.

A white mountain goat statue greets visitors at the park entrance - live ones are common in the region.

WATERTON LAKES NATIONAL PARK

WATERTON LAKES

Waterton Lakes National Park, an out-of-the-way, 528-square-kilometre scenic gem located 265 kilometres south of Calgary, sits on the border with Montana where it joins the U.S. Glacier National Park. Since 1932, the Canadian and American parks, with their common environments, have been linked as the Waterton-Glacier International Peace Park. As the railway never reached Waterton, and as even today no major highway cuts through it, it remains a relatively isolated spot. Central to the park are the magnificent Waterton Lakes, formed during the last ice age 11,000 years ago. Waterton Lake itself is the deepest one in the Canadian Rockies at 150 metres. The park is named after Charles Waterton, an English naturalist born in 1782, who never visited Alberta, but whose writings and work inspired many a 19th-century explorer and scientist.

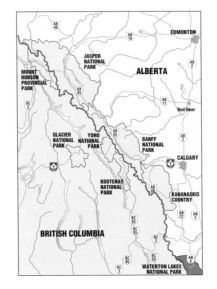

PRINCE OF WALES HOTEL

Local initiatives to preserve the region's beauty led to the creation of the park in 1895. Called Kootenay Lakes Forest Park then, its name changed to Waterton Lakes Dominion Park in 1911. Gradually the little town of Waterton Park developed as a tourist centre. Then, in the 1920s, the Great Northern Railway began offering bus tours through the Rocky Mountains, including Waterton.

The Prince of Wales Hotel opened in 1927 to cater to the bus tour needs for a memorable overnight stop. Today, the 'chalet,' named after the future King Edward VIII (famous for abdicating the throne for the love of Mrs Simpson) is open from mid-May to mid-September. All of the 89 rooms in the seven-storey hotel overlook stunning Waterton Lake.

A popular activity is the boat ride which leaves from the town near the Prince of Wales for a two-hour tour into Montana and back.

This and following pages: the Prince of Wales Hotel, surrounded by wonderful scenery.

CAMERON FALLS

Cameron Falls, in the village of Waterton Park, is a postcard-pretty waterfall which rushes over some of the oldest bedrock in the Rockies. The town itself blossoms during the summer season but becomes a very quiet community of about 100 souls throughout the rest of the year.

Visitors can find the services of a well-equipped tourist centre here during the warm months. The park itself has facilities for camping, boating, fishing, wind surfing, hiking, cycling, horseback riding, as well as such winter endeavours as cross-country skiing, ice climbing, and snowshoeing. Furthermore, some of the best opportunities available for exploring the natural world in Alberta are to be found here: most of the different Rocky Mountain and prairie animals (including bison and elk) live here; the park sits under a major migratory flyway for all kinds of birds during the autumn and spring; and 900 wildflowers and plants - representing half of Alberta's plant species - call Waterton home. However, before you venture off to admire the wildflowers, remember that the Waterton area is known for its cruel winds and sudden storms - so be prepared! Also, most of the tourist services are closed from late September to the middle of May, so Waterton is largely a summer destination except for the hardiest of winter enthusiasts.

Cameron Falls in the Waterton town site.

Cameron Lake, an excellent spot for fishing, boating, and canoeing.

CAMERON LAKE

From the town of Waterton, Cameron Creek runs first northwest, then southwest to Cameron Lake. Parallel to the creek runs the Akamina Parkway through the Cameron Creek Valley, past some of the park's more popular sites. Cameron Lake sits inside a bowl-shaped 'cirque' carved out of the neighbouring mountains by glacial action which created a kind of enormous natural amphitheatre. The south end of the lake sits just inside the American state of Montana and is dominated by the huge Mount Custer there. Custer's slopes are prime grizzly bear country, so keep your eyes open and your guard up. The cold lake is an excellent spot for fishing, boating, and canoeing.

One of the numerous attractions along the 15-kilometre drive from the town to Cameron Lake is the site of Oil City. In 1901 the Rocky Mountain Development Company began drilling for oil here. After 10 months of effort, it struck black gold at 311 metres. Known as Original Discovery No. 1, this was the second oil well in all of Canada, and the first in the western part of the nation. A town grew amidst exalted hopes for wealth, but, after a short time, the promise of massive oil revenues faded and the people left.

Red Rock Canyon, with its brilliantly-coloured argillite.

RED ROCK CANYON

Some of the oldest visible stone in the Rockies can be seen at Waterton, and some of the most interesting of it can be found in Red Rock Canyon where visitors are amazed to encounter the almost lurid red and green argillite. The red is created by oxidized iron particles in the rock while the green is non-oxidized. The canyon itself was created over thousands of years by a small mountain brook which eroded the soft argillite into today's configuration.

To see these and the other engrossing aspects of the region's natural history, follow the Red Rock Canyon Loop Trail. The trail sits 18 kilometres northwest of the Waterton town site along the Red Rock Canyon Parkway which passes by the sharp contrast between mountain and prairie landscapes. Unlike the rest of the Rockies, there are no foothills to separate prairie from mountain here. The trail itself is a very easy, paved, 20-minute walk suitable for families with young children. Furthermore, you are almost certain to encounter some interesting wildlife en route. Over 200 prehistoric sites have been discovered by archaeologists in Waterton Park, including a particularly important one in the Red Rock Canyon dating to 6400 BC.

FAUNA

The Rockies are home to large populations of some of Canada's biggest animals: bighorn sheep, mountain goats, elk, caribou, moose, deer, and bears. The easiest place to see them is along the highways, particularly in the autumn, winter, and spring when many of the bigger animals move from the subalpine forest into the sheltered valleys below. The best, if not the easiest place to encounter wildlife, of course, is in the back country. There, if you're lucky, you might catch a glimpse of rarely seen animals such as cougars, bobcats, lynx, wolverines, pine martens, fishers, otters, flying squirrels, and ermine. Other small creatures which you can view with little difficulty are red squirrels, golden-mantled ground squirrels, the Columbian ground squirrel, beavers, rabbits, porcupines, North America's smallest chipmunk, plus all sorts of songbirds, waterfowl, ground-dwelling birds such as grouse, as well as the great hunting birds, ospreys and eagles.

Elk are the most common of the large animals in much of the Rocky Mountain region, with the Bow River Valley in Banff and the Athabasca River Valley of Jasper being good places to spot them. These giant creatures are about 50 percent larger than a deer. One of the other deer-like animals you can see in the relatively high Sunwapta Valley of Jasper are small bands of caribou, if you visit in winter or spring. (This is the animal on the back of the 25-cent coin.)

Canada's national animal, the beaver, finds a congenial home in low and wet parts of the Rockies, such as the Vermilion Lakes of Banff National Park. This industrious rodent is famous for the dams it builds to create ponds so it can travel safely from its home, a wooden lodge, to its food, consisting mainly of the inner bark of deciduous trees and other vegetation. One of the beaver's most prominent physical features is its large flat tail. If a beaver suspects danger, it slaps its tail on the water's surface to create a loud noise to warn its fellows. The ponds beavers create through their damming activities often are a source of frustration for the animal's human neighbours, but they serve the needs of other beasts, such as moose and deer, who need wetland foods for their survival, as well as the creatures who live in these waters, and the birds and animals who hunt the fish and other pond occupants.

Elk are the most common of the large mammals in the Rockies.

A black bear mother with its cub and a tiny chipmunk, typical creatures of the Canadian Rockies.

Two kinds of bear are common in the Rockies. One is the black bear, the one you are more likely to meet. The other is the grizzly bear, distinguished by a hump behind its shoulders. It is the larger of the two and can run 50 kilometres per hour. Two smaller hunters in the region are the coyote and the wolf. Coyotes are more common and look a bit like foxes. These animals tend to hunt by themselves or in pairs, although they sometimes form packs, particularly during the winter months. Wolves, in contrast, usually chase game in packs of 10 or 12 animals, although some prefer to do it alone - hence the phrase, 'lone wolf.' Today park authorities appreciate that these animals form an important part of the balance of nature. However, that was not always so, and as late as the 1950s attempts were made to eradicate coyotes and wolves from Banff.

Mountain goats can be seen in Jasper. These white animals with their black horns normally live at higher elevations, although sometimes you will see them foraging down in the valleys to lick clay to meet their need for nutrients. They are famous for their ability to climb staggeringly difficult mountains from the first day of their birth. Whether from the highway or in rough country, early morning or evening before sunset are the best times to see and photograph animals. Cute and furry as they are, it is important to remember that these are wild animals. Keep your distance to avoid tragedy! Also, remember that it is illegal to feed the wildlife. If given the chance, they will fill up on junk food rather than eat enough of the right foods to enable them to survive in the harsh Rocky Mountain climate.

As well, they occasionally become dangerous nuisances in their quest for easy handouts which sometimes forces park officials to destroy them.

An elk with the Rockies in the background.

Especially in spring and autumn it's easy to meet an elk along the highways.

A large black bear.

FLORA

The Canadian Rockies are the home of a tremendous variety of flowers and plants. Some are common to the region as a whole; others are unique to specific areas because peculiar local ecosystems support wildlife that would not survive elsewhere.

There are four typical ecological zones in the region, the montane forest, the subalpine forest, the alpine tundra, and looming over all, the frozen tops of the taller mountains. The lower regions of montane forest contain various trees, the dominant ones being Douglas fir, white spruce, lodgepole, limber pine, trembling aspen, and balsam fir. Above this region is the subalpine forest, the home of spruce, subalpine fir, Lyall's larch, and white-bark pine trees. (Lyall's larches are particularly interesting. Unlike most other coniferous trees, they lose their needles after turning gold and yellow in the autumn. These slow-growing trees - many of them hundreds of years old - shed their needles in order to conserve the meagre supply of nutrients they can pull out of the local soil.)

Above the subalpine forest is the area of alpine tundra, a region marked by its magnificent flowers which prosper in these dry, windswept regions. One of the tough but delightful flowers you'll see up there is Moss Campion, which grows densely and is marked by its bright green leaves and tiny pink flowers. This plant is particularly good at retaining moisture and breaking down rocks to create soil. Thus, it often is the first to appear in the higher regions after a rockslide. However, like many alpine plants, it grows slowly, taking as long as 20 years to bloom. As well, keep an eye out for such plants as the Glacier Lily with its yellow flowers; Paintbrush with purple, yellow, and cream flowers; and Mountain Heather with bell-shaped flowers in white, yellow, and pink. Finally, rising over the other ecological zones, is the cold and desolate world of the mountain top. All in all, the Canadian Rockies are the place to go if you're a flower and plant enthusiast because you have the opportunity to search out and enjoy 53 different liverworts, 407 kinds of lichen, 243 mosses, and 996 vascular plants such as trees, grasses, and flowers.

Some of the floral glories of the Canadian Rockies.

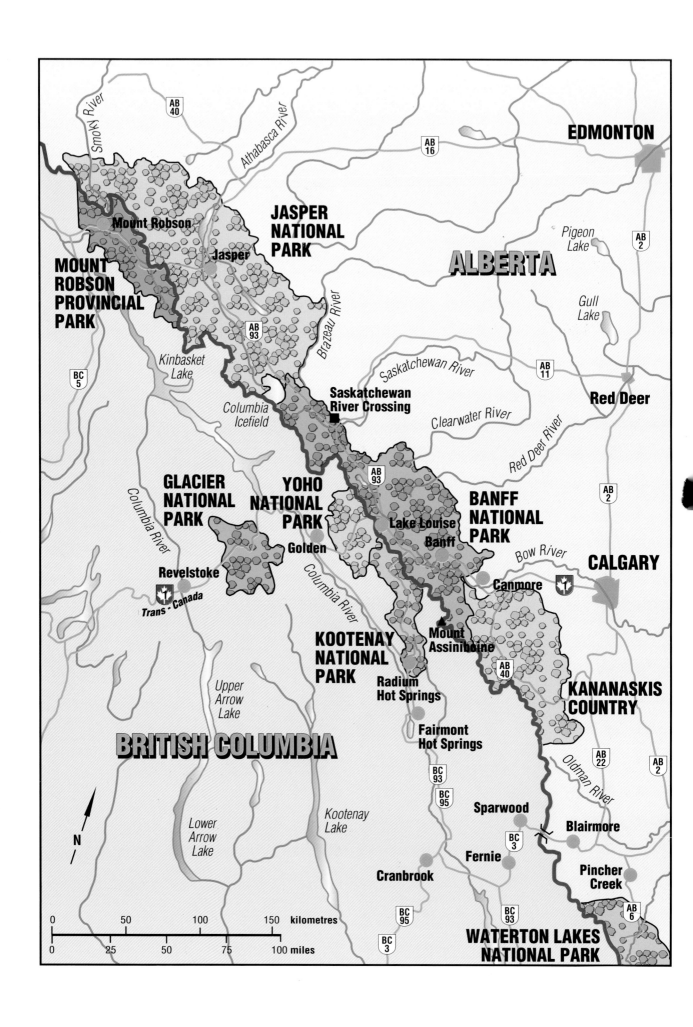